DRAW 50

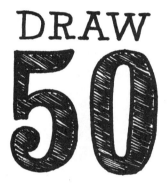

DOGS

The Step-by-Step Way to Draw Beagles,
German Shepherds, Collies,
Golden Retrievers, Yorkies, Pugs,
Malamutes, and Many More . . .

BOOKS IN THIS SERIES

- *Draw 50 Airplanes, Aircraft, and Spacecraft*
- *Draw 50 Aliens*
- *Draw 50 Animal 'Toons*
- *Draw 50 Animals*
- *Draw 50 Athletes*
- *Draw 50 Baby Animals*
- *Draw 50 Beasties*
- *Draw 50 Birds*
- *Draw 50 Boats, Ships, Trucks, and Trains*
- *Draw 50 Buildings and Other Structures*
- *Draw 50 Cars, Trucks, and Motorcycles*
- *Draw 50 Cats*
- *Draw 50 Creepy Crawlies*
- *Draw 50 Dinosaurs and Other Prehistoric Animals*
- *Draw 50 Dogs*
- *Draw 50 Endangered Animals*
- *Draw 50 Famous Cartoons*
- *Draw 50 Flowers, Trees, and Other Plants*
- *Draw 50 Horses*
- *Draw 50 Magical Creatures*
- *Draw 50 Monsters*
- *Draw 50 People*
- *Draw 50 Princesses*
- *Draw 50 Sharks, Whales, and Other Sea Creatures*
- *Draw 50 Vehicles*
- *Draw the Draw 50 Way*

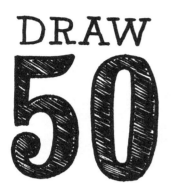

DRAW 50 DOGS

The Step-by-Step Way to Draw Beagles, German Shepherds, Collies, Golden Retrievers, Yorkies, Pugs, Malamutes, and Many More . . .

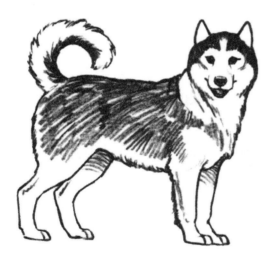

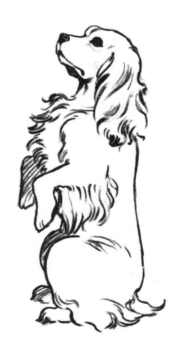

LEE J. AMES

Watson-Guptill Publications, New York

Library of Congress Cataloging-in-Publication Data

Ames, Lee J.
    Draw 50 dogs/ Lee J. Ames.
    Summary: Provides step-by-step instruction for drawing fifty
different breeds of dogs.
    p. cm.
1. Dogs in art—2. Drawing—Technique. [1.Dogs in art. 2. Drawing—
Technique] 1. Title. II. Title:
Draw 50 dogs
NC780.A483 1986
743/ .6074442
                                79006853
Captions courtesy of The Gaines People Guide to America's
Dogs wall chart.
Reprinted by permission.

ISBN 978-0-8230-8583-5
eISBN 978-0-7704-3290-4

Printed in the United States of America

10 9 8 7 6 5 4 3 2 1

TO BUTCHIE DELL AMES, LE MAY'S RED WHATTIS (TINY),
AND SAM (NÉE RESTLESS)

and thanks again to Holly Moylan, super-helper

TO THE READER

This book will show you a way to draw dogs. You need not start with the first illustration. Choose whichever you wish. When you have decided, follow the step-by-step method shown. **Very lightly** and **carefully** sketch out step number one. This step, which is the easiest, should be done **most carefully.** Step number two is added right to step number one, also done lightly and very carefully. Step number three is sketched right on top of numbers one and two. Continue in this way to the last step.

It may seem strange to ask you to be extra careful when you are drawing what seem to be the easiest first steps, but this is most important, for a careless mistake at the beginning may spoil the whole picture at the end. As you sketch out each step, watch the spaces between the lines, as well as the lines, and see that they are the same. After each step, you may want to lighten your work by pressing it with a kneaded eraser (available at art supply stores).

When you have finished, you may want to redo the final step in India ink with a fine brush or pen. When the ink is dry, use the kneaded eraser to remove the pencil lines. The eraser will not affect the India ink.

Here are some suggestions: In the first few steps, even when all seems quite correct, you might do well to hold your work up to a mirror. Sometimes the mirror shows that you've twisted the drawing off to one side without being aware of it. At first you may find it difficult to draw the egg shapes, or ball shapes, or sausage shapes, or to just make the pencil go where you wish. Don't be discouraged. The more you practice, the more you will develop control.

The only equipment you'll need will be a medium or soft pencil, paper, the kneaded eraser and, if you wish, a pen or brush.

The first steps in this book are shown darker than necessary so that they can be clearly seen. (Keep your work very light.)

Remember, there are many other ways and methods to make drawings. This book shows just one method. Why don't you seek out other ways from teachers, from libraries and, most importantly, from inside yourself?

Lee J. Ames

TO THE PARENT OR TEACHER

"David can draw a collie better than anybody else!" Such peer acclaim and encouragement generate incentive. Contemporary methods of art instruction (freedom of expression, experimentation, self-evaluation of competence and growth) provide a vigorous, fresh-air approach for which we must all be grateful.

New ideas need not, however, totally exclude the old. One such idea is the "follow-me-step-by-step" approach. In my young learning days this method was so common, and frequently so exclusive, that the student became nothing more than a pantographic extension of the teacher. In those days it was excessively overworked.

This does not mean that the young hand is never to be guided. Rather, specific guiding is fundamental. Step-by-step guiding that produces satisfactory results is valuable even when the means of accomplishment are not fully understood by the student.

The novice with a musical instrument is frequently taught to play simple melodies as quickly as possible, well before he learns the most elemental scratchings at the surface of music theory. The resultant self-satisfaction, pride in accomplishment, can be a significant means of providing motivation. And all from mimicking an instructor's "Do-as-I-do."

Mimicry is a prerequisite for developing creativity.

We learn how to use our tools by means of mimicry. Then we can use those tools for creativity. To this end, I would offer the budding artist the opportunity to memorize or mimic (rotelike, if you wish) the making of "pictures" he has been anxious to draw.

The use of this book should in no way be compulsory. Rather, it should be available to anyone who **wants** to try another way of developing skills. Perhaps he will then be encouraged to produce more significant accomplishments when his friend says, "David can draw a collie better than anybody else!"

Lee J. Ames

The Hound Breeds

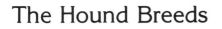

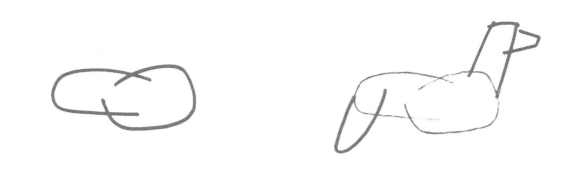

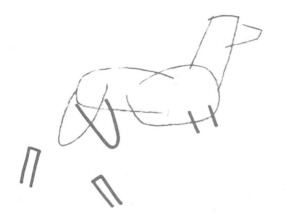

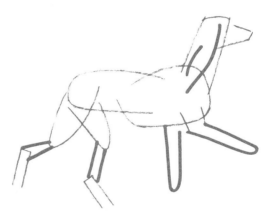

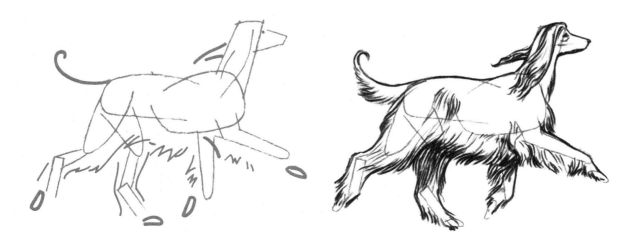

AFGHAN HOUND

Pictured in rock carvings of Afghanistan dating back 4000 years, once used to pursue gazelles.
Av. wt. 60 lbs., ht. 27″. Coat: long. Color: usually tan, black, fawn, cream, blue.

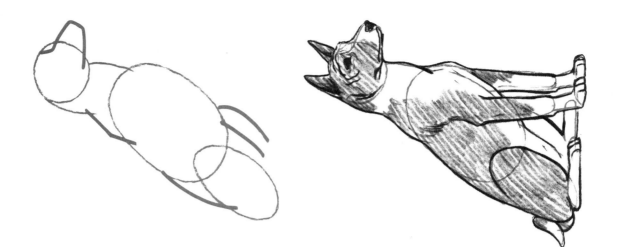

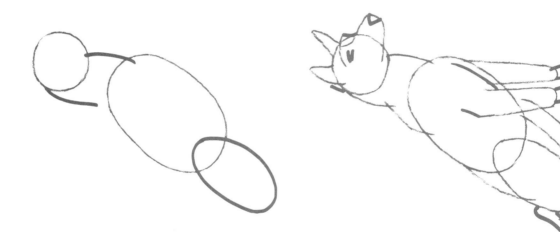

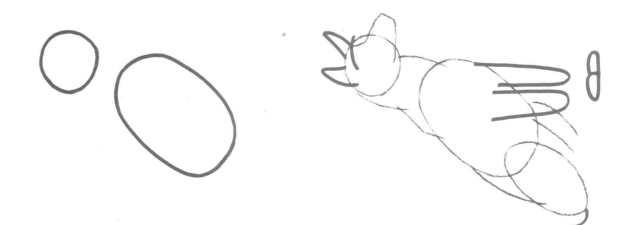

BASENJI
Known as the "barkless dog." A hunter in its native African Congo, first brought to U.S. in 1937.
Av. wt. 22 lbs., ht. 16″. Coat: short, silky. Color: red, black, black and tan, all with white markings.

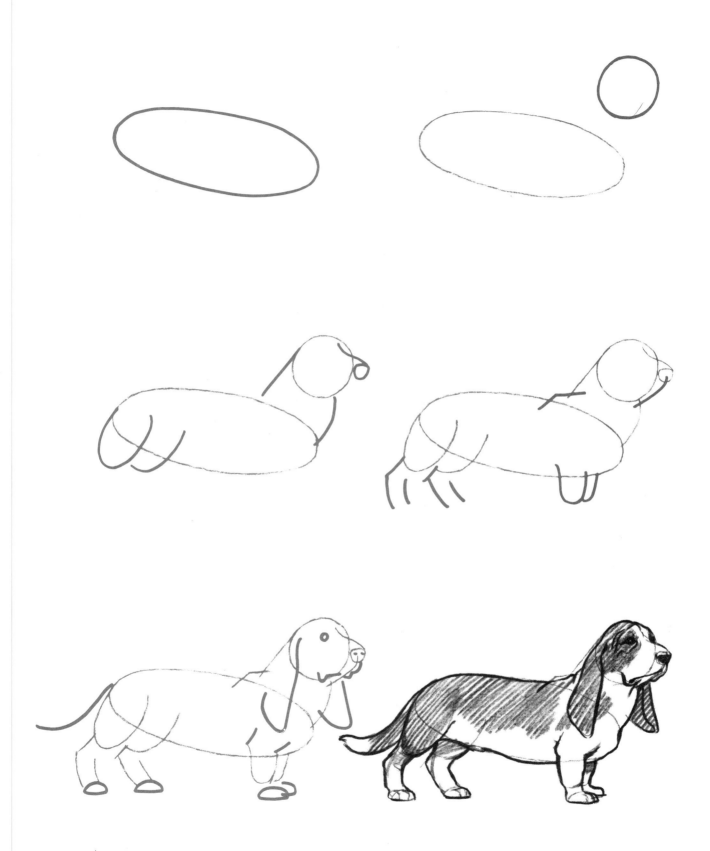

BASSET HOUND

From ancient French hounds used for slow trailing of game. One of America's oldest breeds.
Av. wt. 50 lbs., ht. 14″. Coat: short. Color: black, tan, white; any hound color.

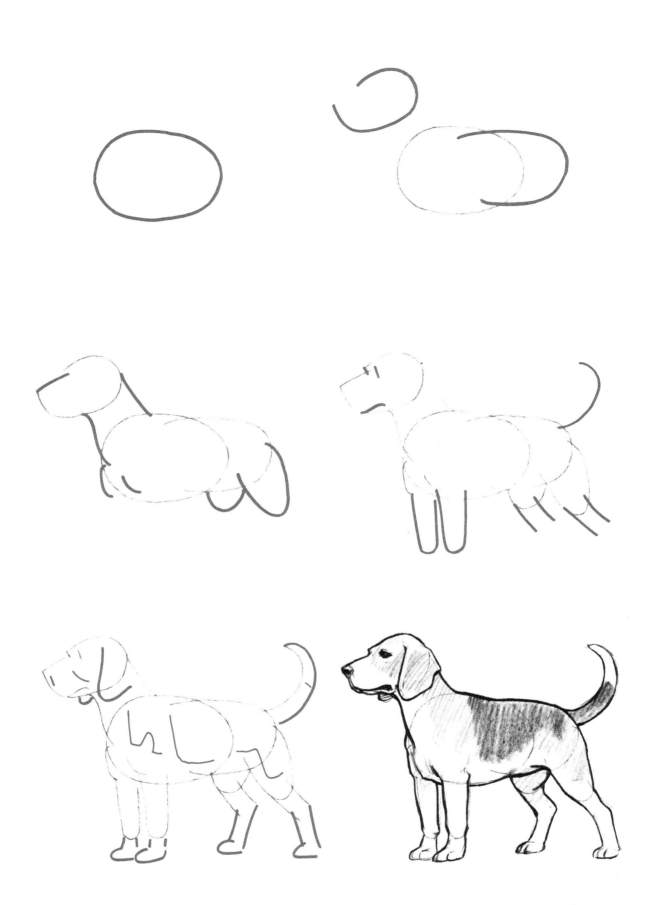

BEAGLE

From England and long popular in America; hunters' favorite for rabbit and hare. 2 sizes: under 13″, wt. 18 lbs.; over 13–15″, 30 lbs. Coat: short. Color: white, black, tan; any hound color.

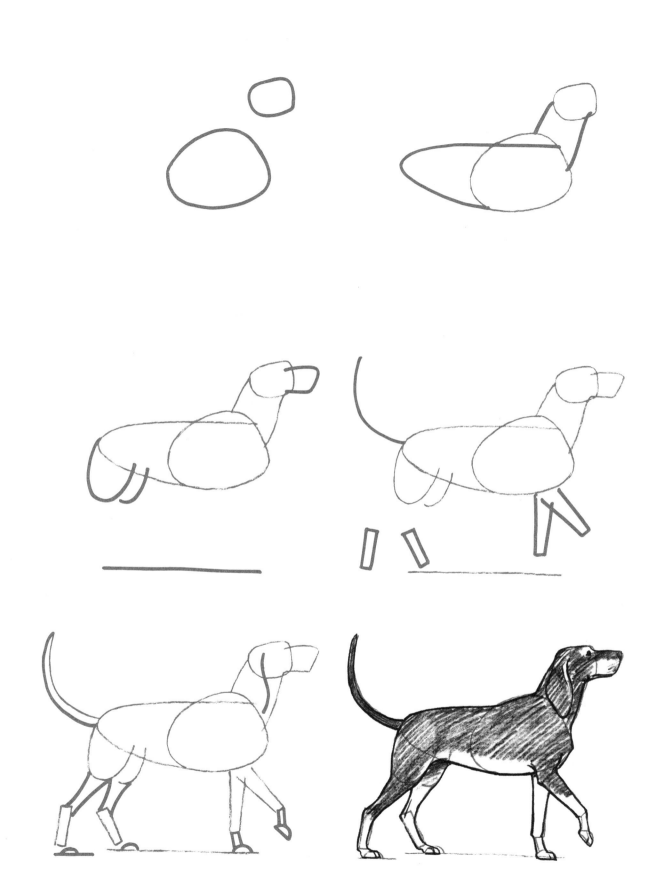

BLACK AND TAN COONHOUND
Descended from hounds of 11th-century England, this type developed from Virginia hounds of early settlers. Av. wt. 60 lbs., ht. 25″. Coat: short. Color: black, tan markings.

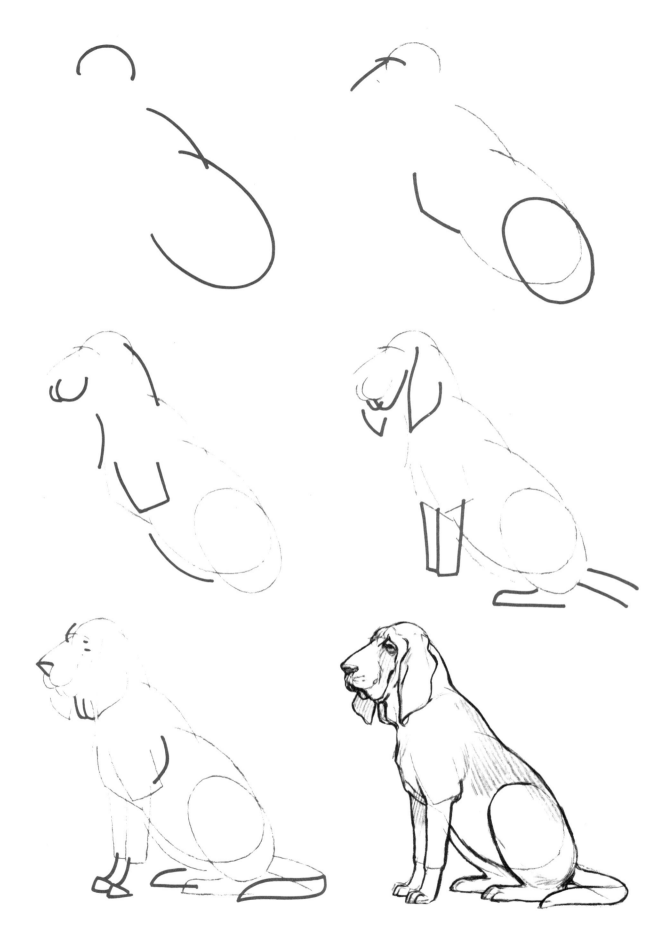

BLOODHOUND
Oldest trailing breed. Records kept in the 12th century prompted name of "blooded hounds." In America over a century. Av. wt. 90 lbs., ht. 26″. Coat: short. Color: black or red and tan, tawny.

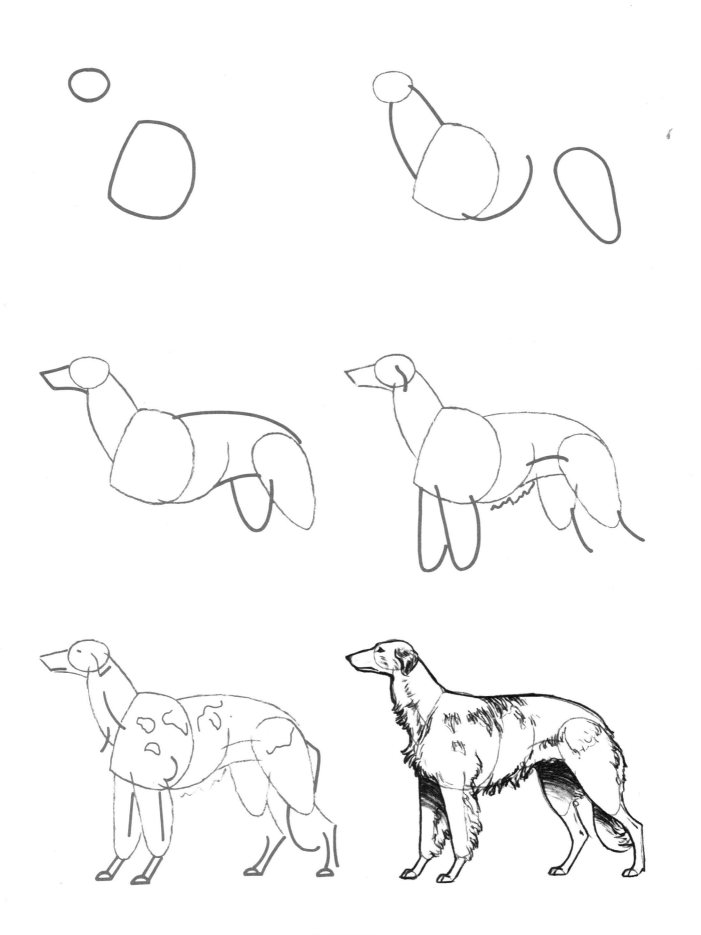

BORZOI

Formerly called Russian wolfhounds, used in Czarist Russia to chase wolves. In U.S. since 1889.
Av. wt. 90 lbs., ht. 30″. Coat: long, wavy. Color: any color or combination of colors.

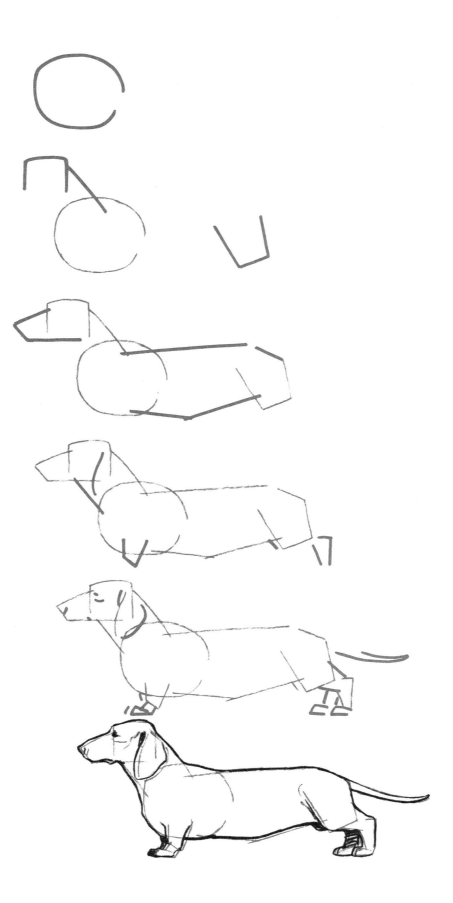

DACHSHUND

German name meaning "badger dog" for ancestors that fought the vicious badger underground.
Highly popular as pet. Av. wt. 20 lbs., ht. 9″. Standard and Miniature (under 10 lbs.). Coat: smooth.

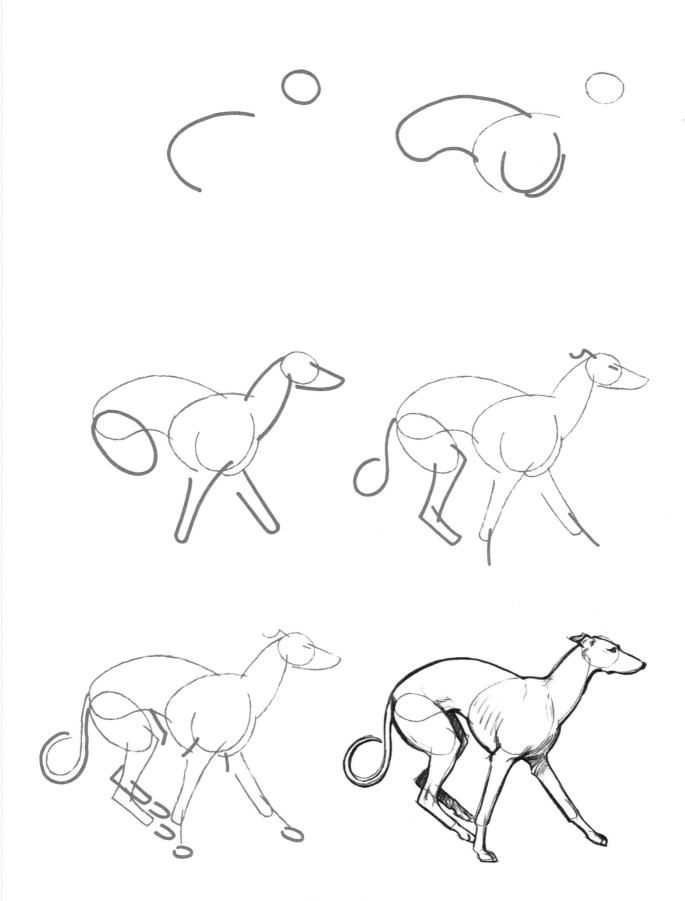

GREYHOUND
This canine symbol of speed coursed gazelle in Egypt 4000 years ago and was royalty's favorite in early Greece and Rome. Av. wt. 65 lbs., ht. 26″. Coat: smooth. Color: any color.

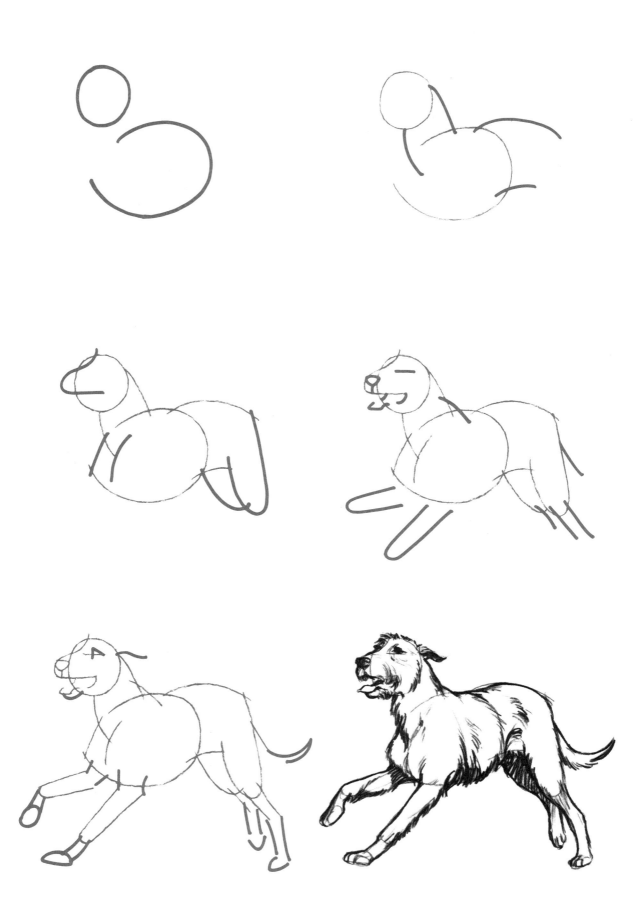

IRISH WOLFHOUND

Tallest of the breeds, used in feudal Middle Ages to hunt wolves and elk. Brought to America in 1800s. Av. wt. 130 lbs., ht. 33″. Coat: harsh. Color: gray, brindle, tan, black, white.

The Terriers

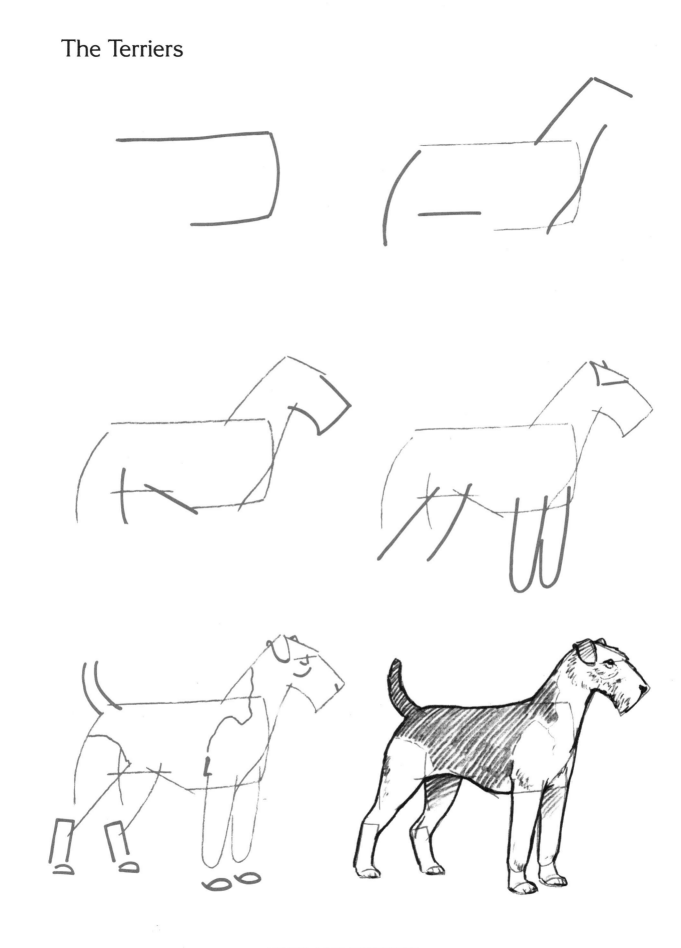

AIREDALE TERRIER
Originally used for hunting otter, other small game in England. Height of popularity in U.S. 1905–20. Av. wt. 50 lbs., ht. 23″. Coat: harsh, wiry. Color: tan, black back, sides.

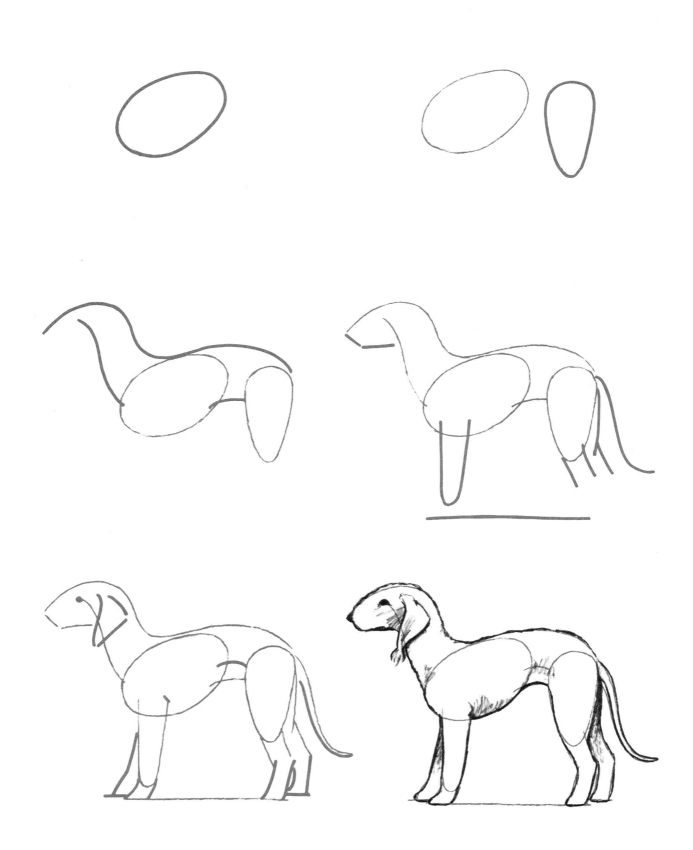

BEDLINGTON TERRIER
Named for English coal region where used in 19th century as ratter. Av. wt. 23 lbs., ht. 16″.
Coat: thick, soft, trimmed to smooth appearance. Color: blue-gray, tan, liver.

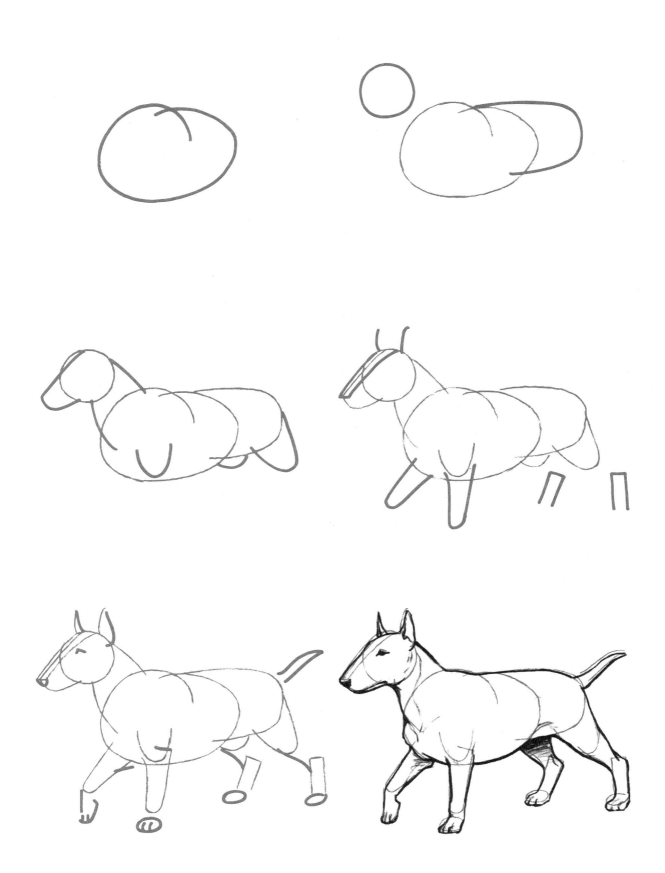

BULL TERRIER
Developed in England 100 years ago. Fashionable pet used for fighting by sporting gentry.
Av. wt. 50 lbs., ht. 20″. Coat: short. Color: white; also seen in brindle colored variety.

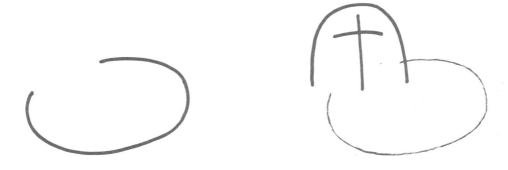

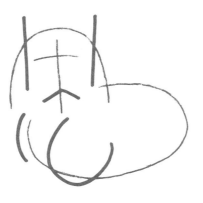

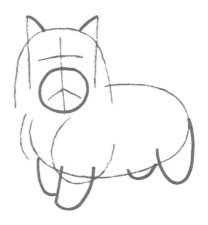

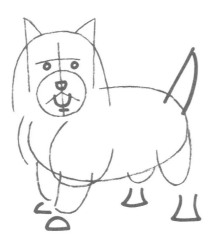

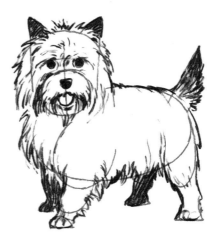

CAIRN TERRIER

Rugged working terrier of Scotland, named for rocky piles into which it burrowed after game.
Av. wt. 14 lbs., ht. 10″. Coat: harsh, soft undercoat. Color: usually wheaten, tan, and grizzle.

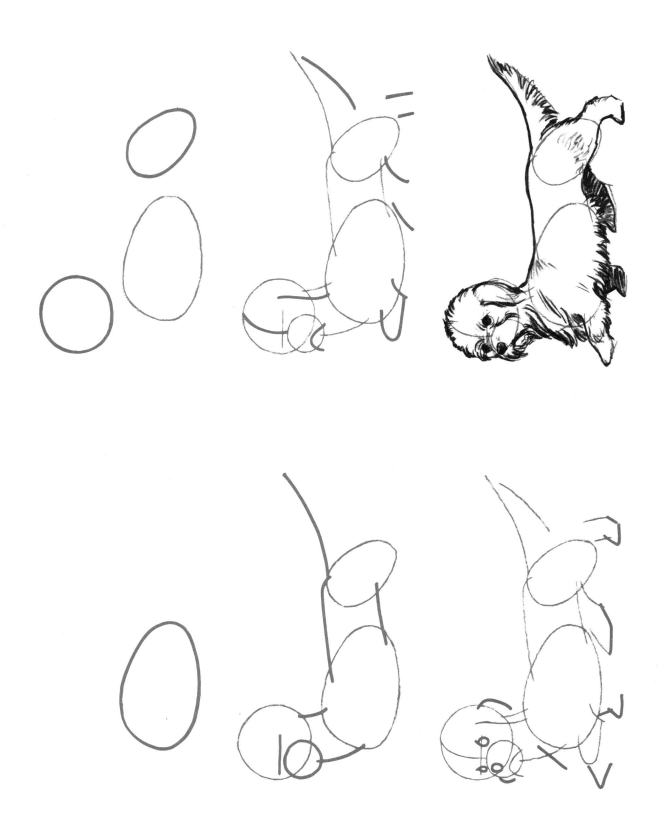

DANDIE DINMONT TERRIER

Hunting terrier of Scottish border, named after character in Scott's **Guy Mannering.** Av. wt. 22 lbs., ht. 10". Coat: medium length. Color: pepper-and-salt, mustard.

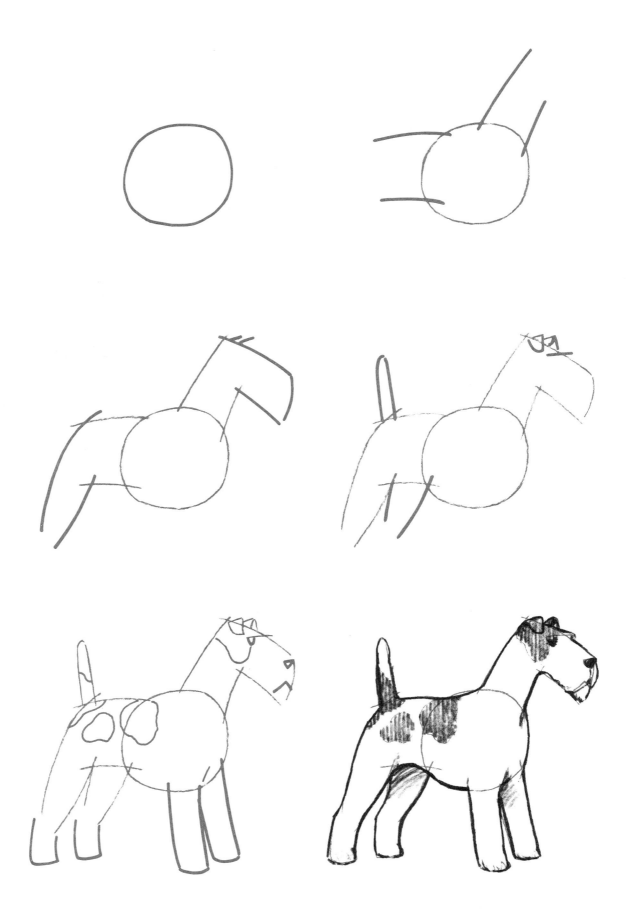

FOX TERRIER (WIRE)

Early English Terrier used to dig out foxes. Long popular in U.S., particularly in '20s. Av. wt. 17 lbs., ht. 15″. Coat: wiry, close. Color: white with black or tan markings, or both.

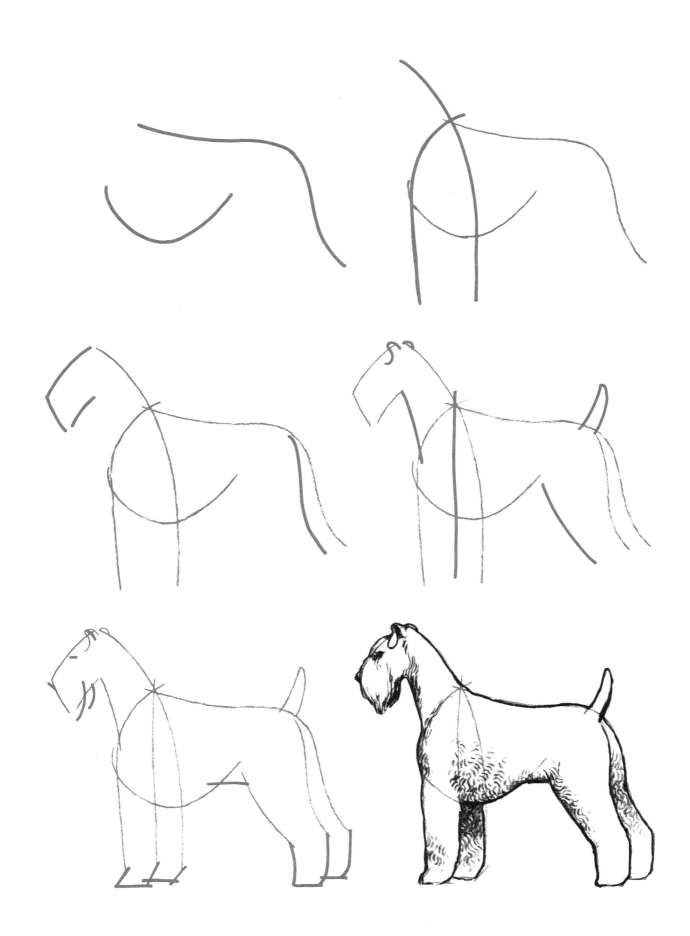

KERRY BLUE TERRIER
From Kerry mountain country, used as farm and hunting dog. National dog of Ireland. Av. wt. 35 lbs., ht. 18″. Coat: dense, wavy. Color: gunmetal to steel blue.

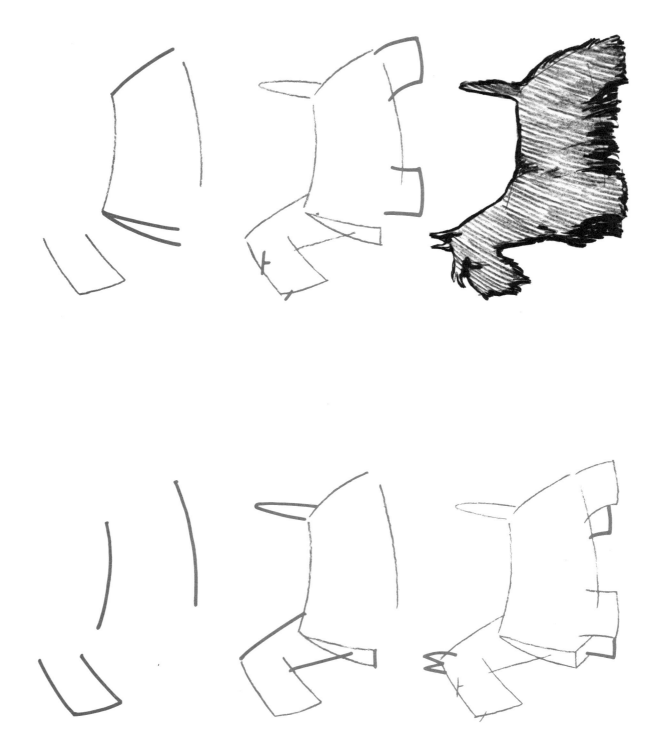

SCOTTISH TERRIER

Highland terrier, ancestor of all other terriers of Scotland. "Scotty" popular in U.S. a century.
Av. wt. 20 lbs., ht. 10″. Coat: thick and wiry. Color: black, sandy or grizzle, gray.

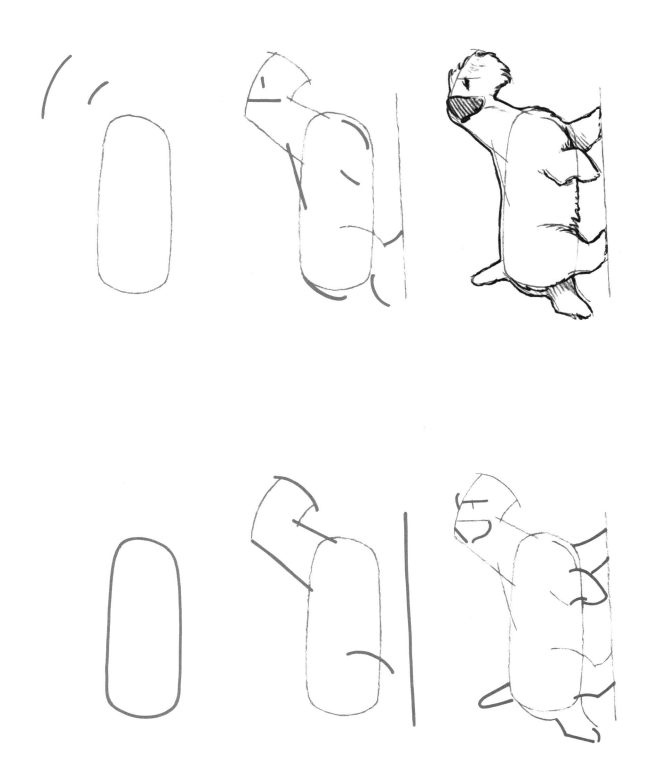

SEALYHAM TERRIER

Named for Welsh origin, another badger, otter and fox-hunter. Short-legged with docked tail.
Av. wt. 20 lbs., ht. 10″. Coat: wiry, double. Color: white, or with tan ears.

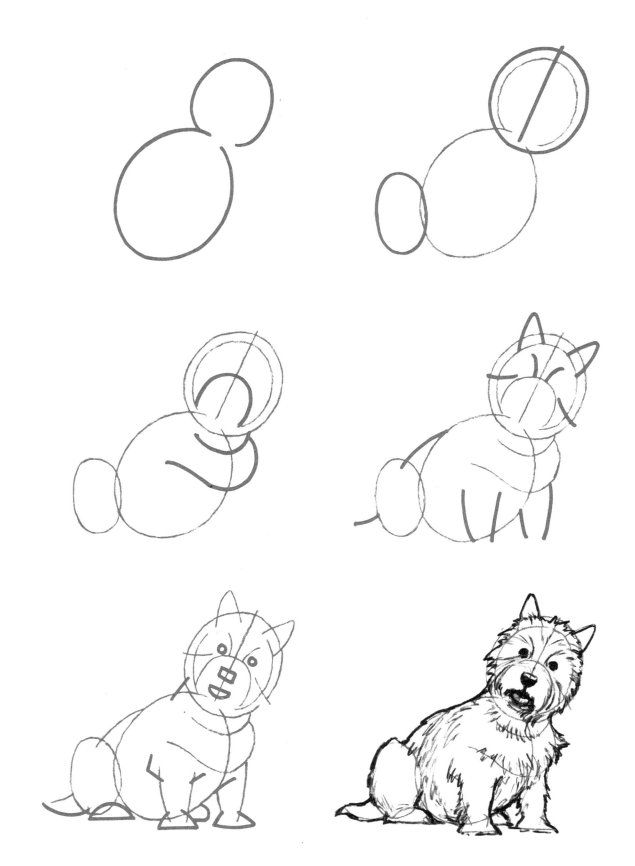

WEST HIGHLAND WHITE TERRIER
Originated by Duke of Argyll. Was first named Roseneath after his estate. Similar to foxy Scotty.
Av. wt. 16 lbs., ht. 10″. Coat: hard, thick. Color: white.

The Working Breeds

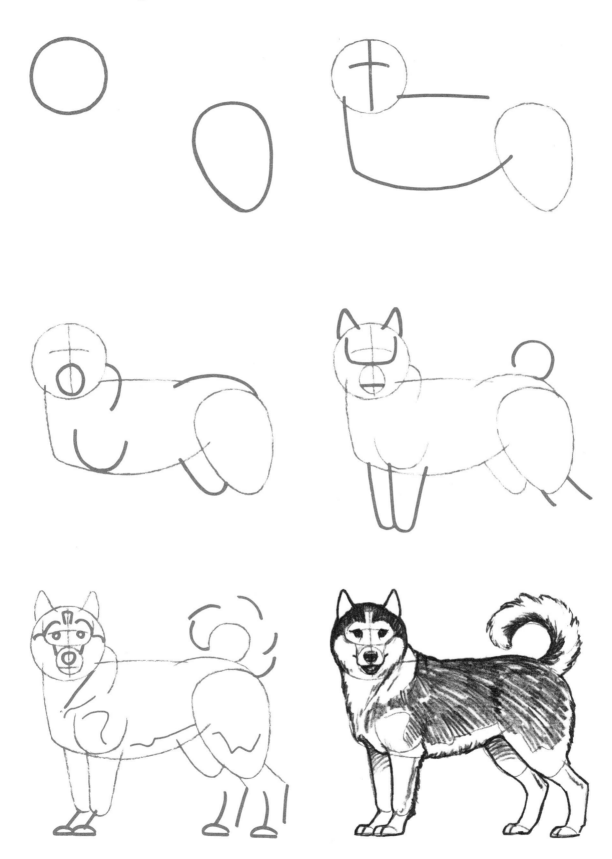

ALASKAN MALAMUTE
Named for Malamute tribe, used for centuries in North as beast of burden. Av. wt. 85 lbs., ht. 24″.
Coat: thick. Color: gray to black, white undercoat, mask or cap on face.

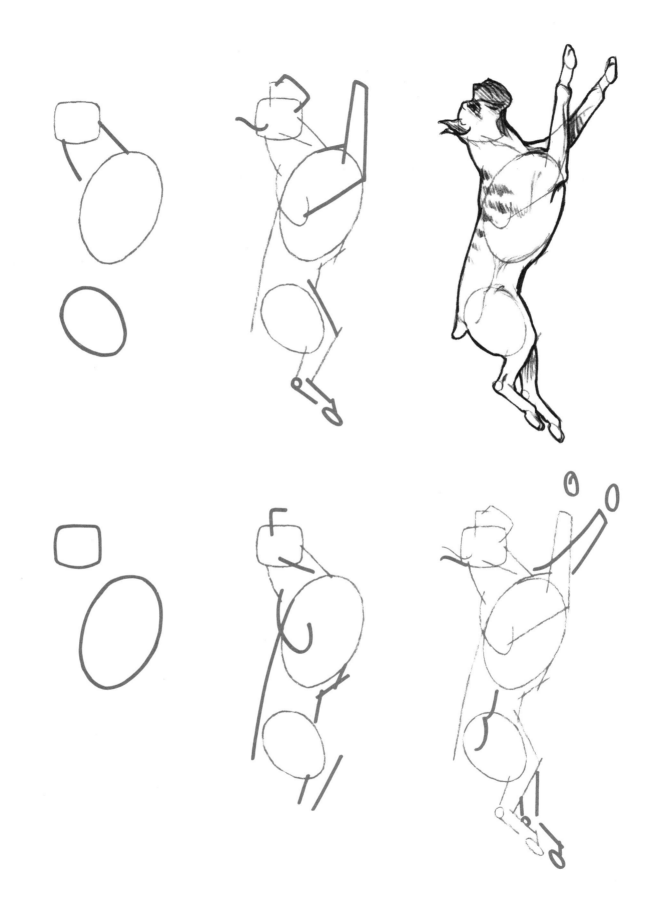

BOXER

From Germany, named for way of using paws in playing. Began rise to popularity in U.S. during 1930s. Av. wt. 70 lbs., ht. 23″. Coat: short, smooth. Color: fawn or brindle, solid or with white.

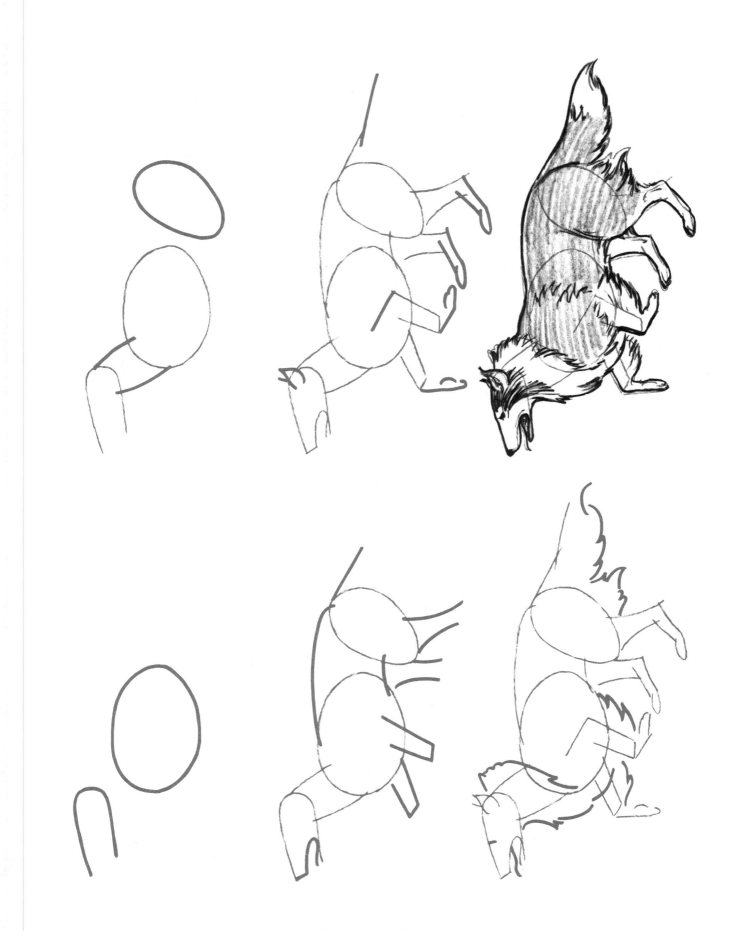

COLLIE (ROUGH)

Herding dog of Scotland for centuries, for 80 years one of America's most popular breeds.
Av. wt. 65 lbs., ht. 24″. Coat: abundant. Color: sable, white, tricolor, blue merle.

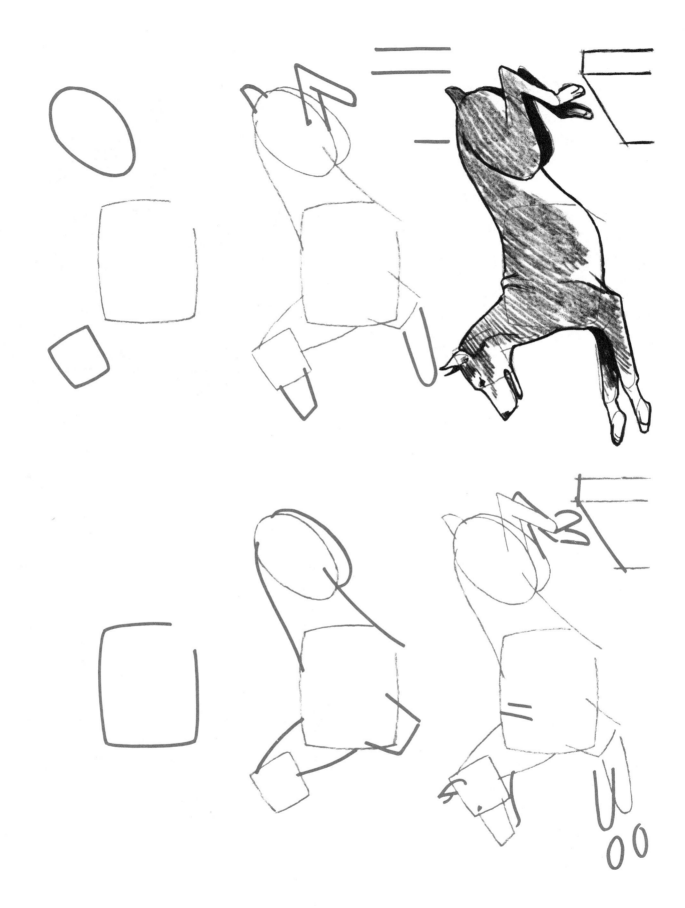

DOBERMAN PINSCHER

Official war dog of U.S. Marines, distinguished in World War II. Developed in Germany. Av. wt. 70 lbs., ht. 27″. Coat: short, smooth. Color: black or red with rust, blue, fawn.

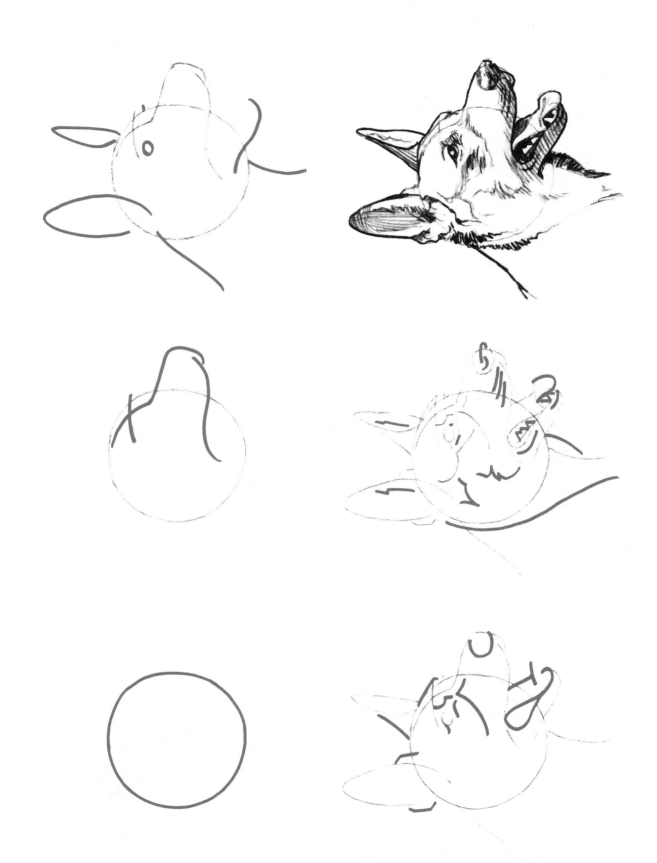

GERMAN SHEPHERD DOG
Heroism in World War I began popularity in U.S., where renowned as guide and army dog.
Av. wt. 75 lbs., ht. 25″. Coat: dense. Color: black-and-tan, gray, various rich browns.

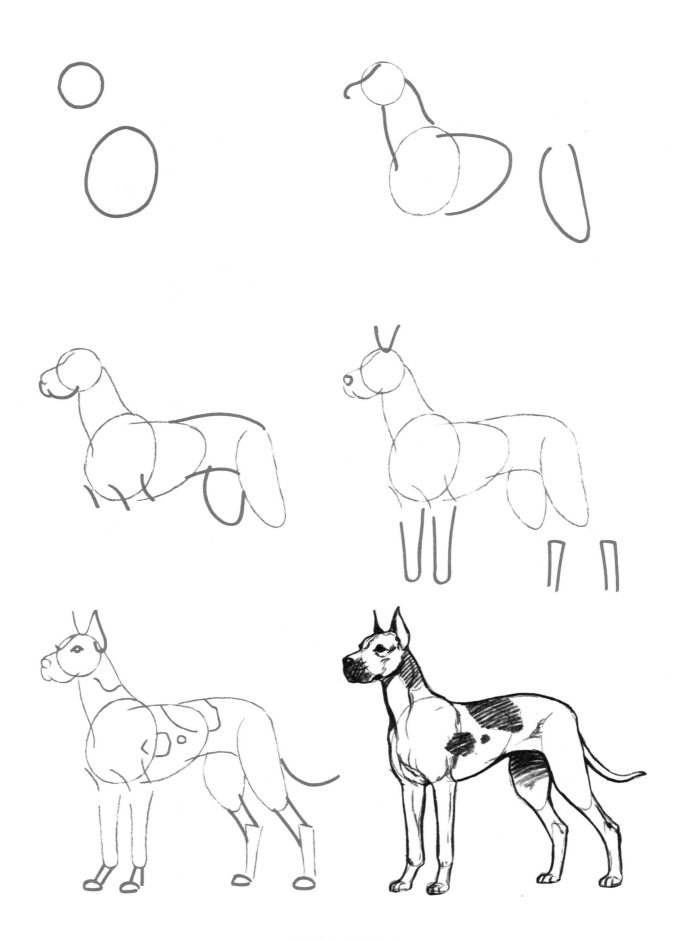

GREAT DANE
Originated in Germany 400 years ago as boar hunter. Known as the Apollo of dogdom. Av. wt. 130 lbs., ht. 32″. Coat: smooth. Color: brindle, fawn, blue, black, harlequin (black and white).

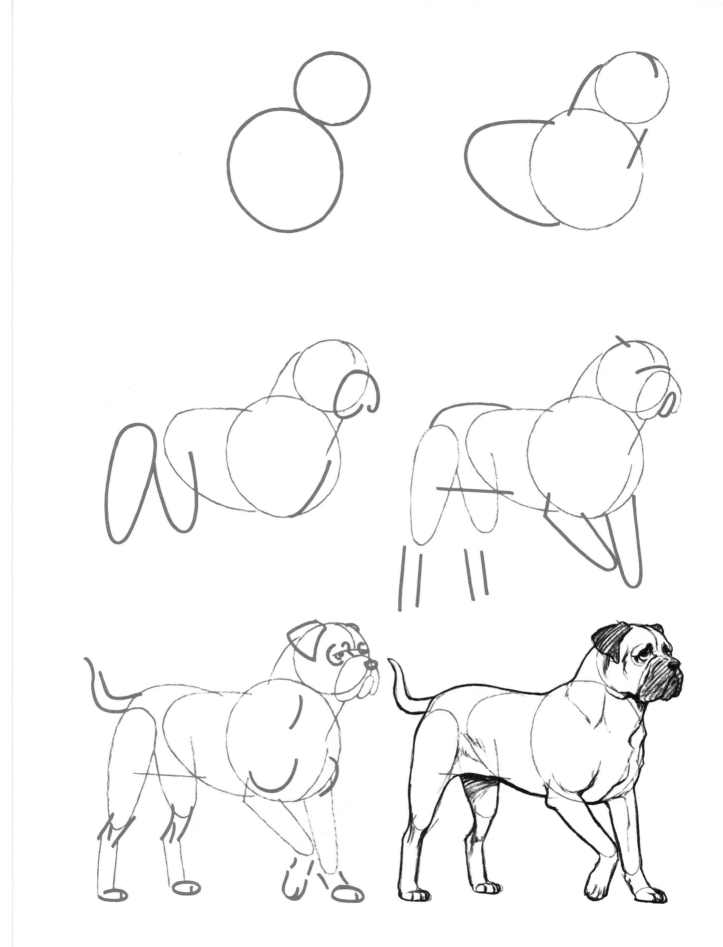

MASTIFF

In England for centuries, used as guards. In 55 B.C. Roman invaders took many back to Rome.
Brought to America by early settlers. Av. wt. 185 lbs., ht. 32″. Coat: short. Color: fawn, brindle.

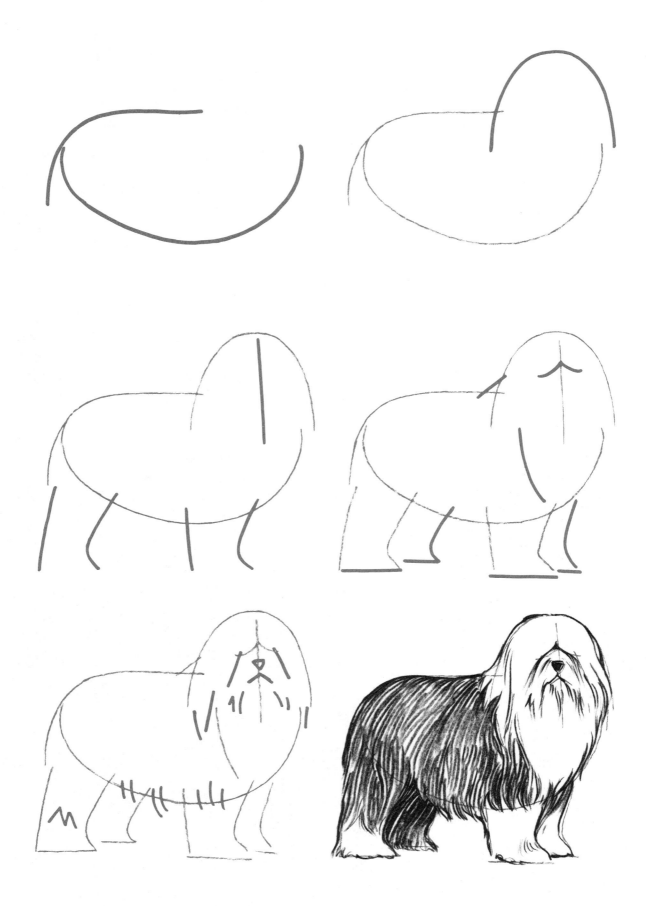

OLD ENGLISH SHEEPDOG

England's drovers' dog, with rolling, bearlike gait, once called "Bobtail." Av. wt. 95 lbs., ht. 24".
Coat: long: Color: shades of "pigeon blue," with or without white markings.

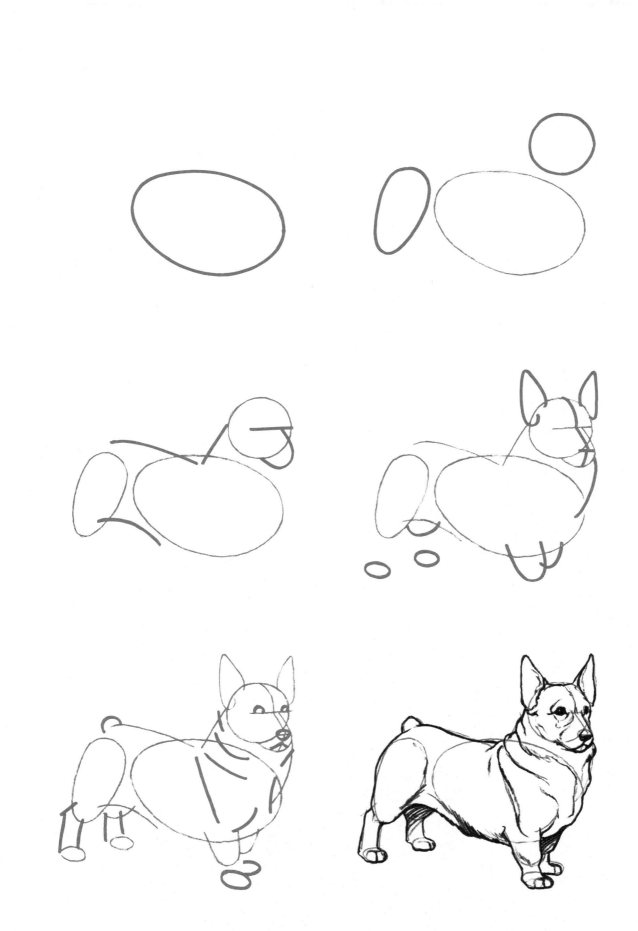

PEMBROKE WELSH CORGI
Ancient breed of Wales, descended from dogs of Flemish weavers. Docked tail. Av. wt. 25 lbs.,
ht. 11″. Coat: short. Color: red, fawn, black and tan, with or without white markings.

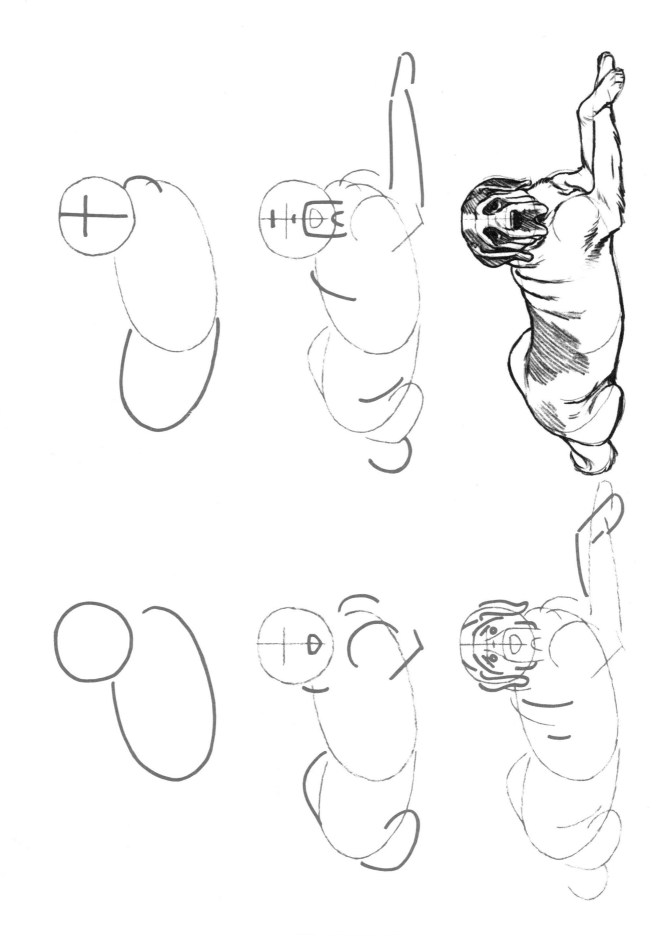

ST. BERNARD

Rescue dog of Swiss Alps, saver of thousands of lives in 300 years' use at St. Bernard Hospice.
Av. wt. 165 lbs., ht. 28″. Coat: long or short. Color: white with red or brindle.

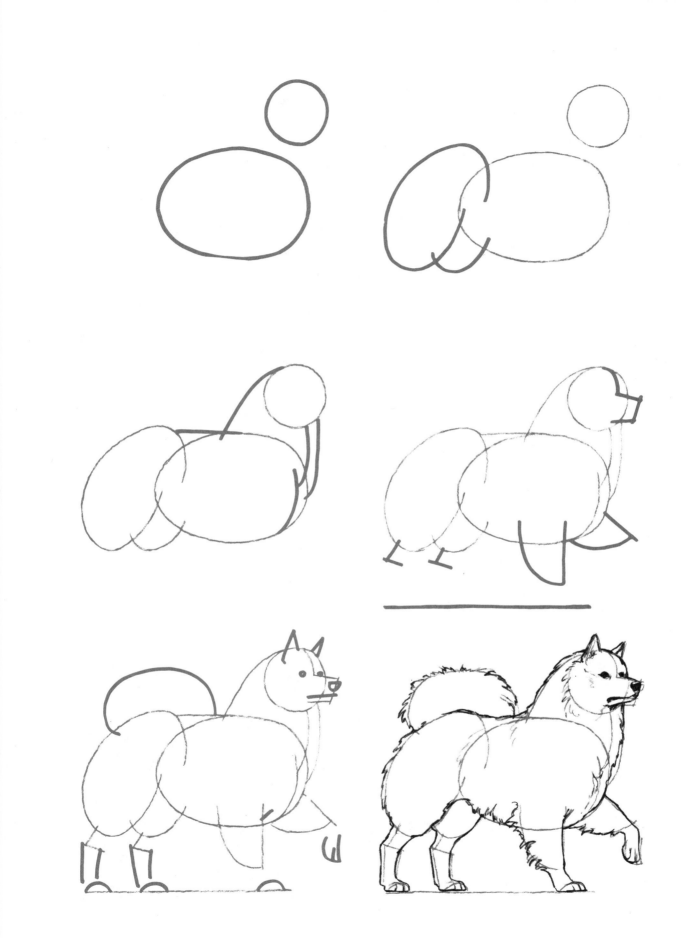

SAMOYED
Named for nomadic Arctic tribe of Siberia, where it served as pet, sled dog, reindeer herder.
Brought to England by explorers 100 years ago. Av. wt. 55 lbs., ht. 22″. Coat: thick. Color: white.

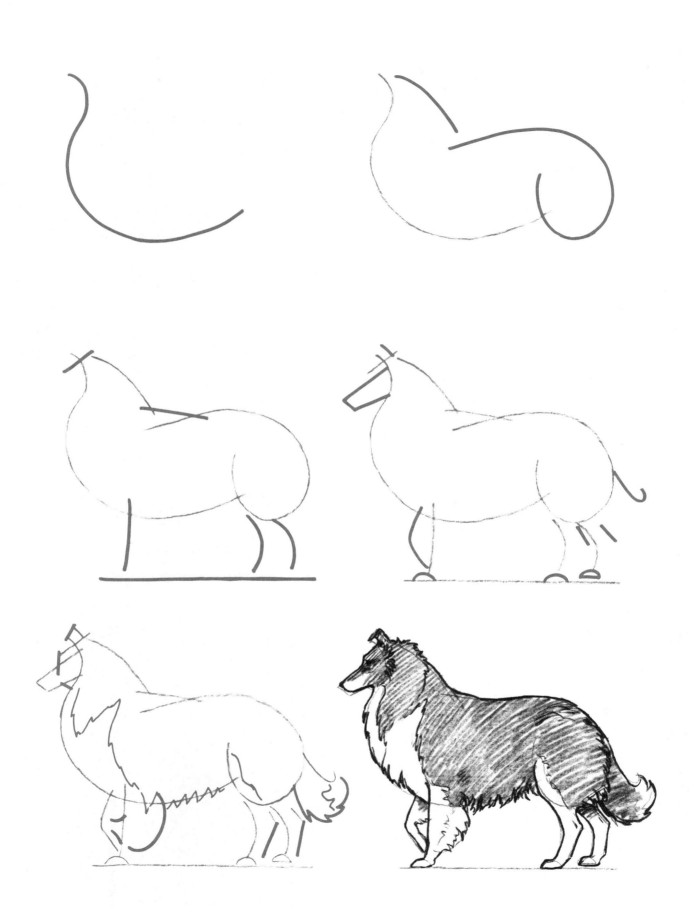

SHETLAND SHEEPDOG

From Shetland Isles, where all animals are small. Collie in miniature, nicknamed Sheltie. Av. wt. 16 lbs., ht. 14″. Coat: long, heavy. Color: sable and white, tricolor, blue.

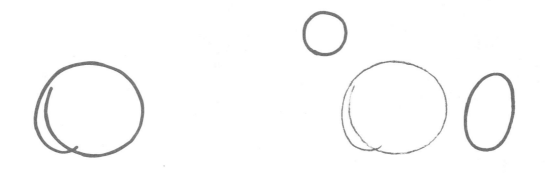

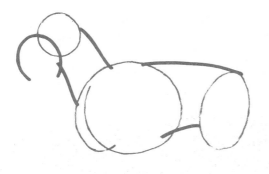

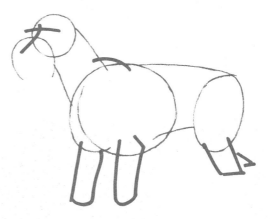

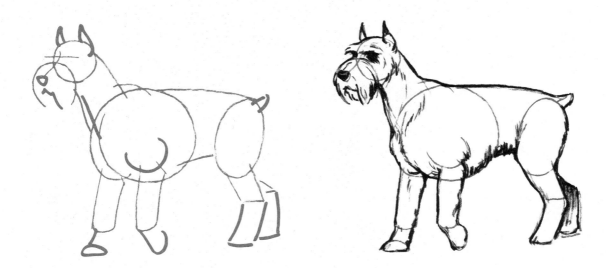

STANDARD SCHNAUZER
Popular in Germany since 15th century as ratter, farm guard. In America since 1899, but not well known. Av. wt. 35 lbs., ht. 19″. Coat: wiry. Color: black, pepper-and-salt.

The Sporting Breeds

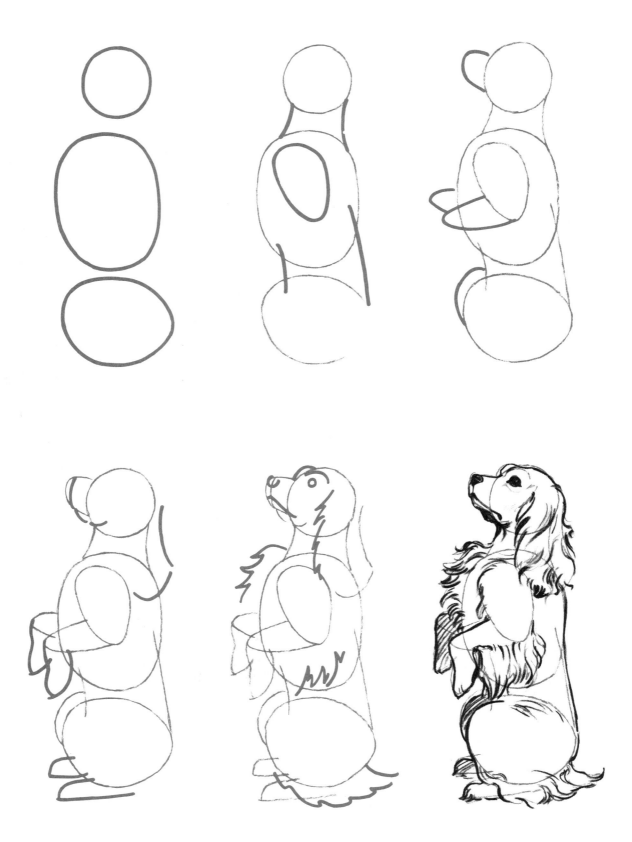

COCKER SPANIEL

With name, from early use in England on woodcock, long among America's favorites. Av. wt. 25 lbs., ht. 14″. Coat: wavy. Color: 3 varieties—solid black, red, buff, black with tan, parti-color.

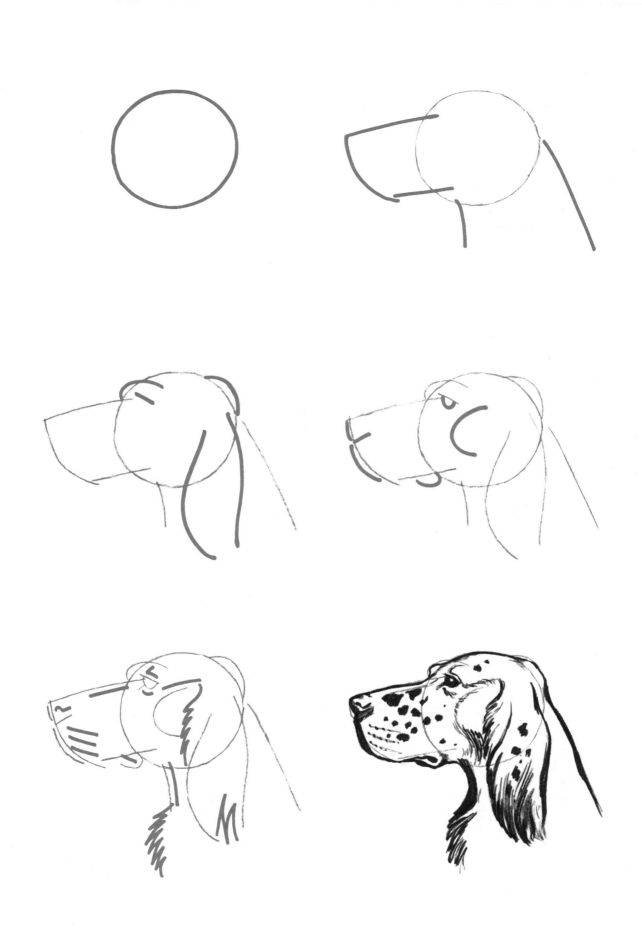

ENGLISH SETTER

Used in England on game birds 400 years. Highly favored by American sportsmen since 1874. Av. wt. 65 lbs., ht. 25″. Coat: long. Color: white with black, lemon, orange, blue.

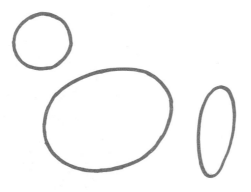
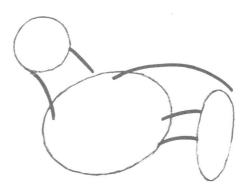
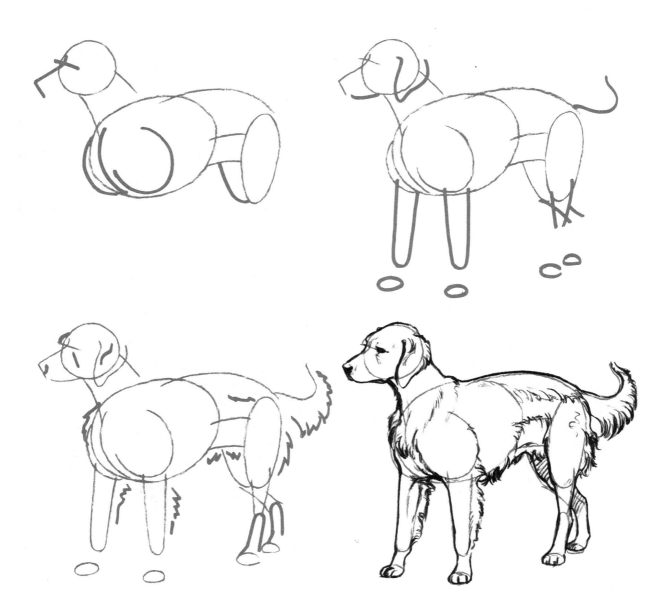

GOLDEN RETRIEVER
Developed from retrievers in England, but distinguished by coat and color. Known in America since 1932. Av. wt. 70 lbs., ht. 23″. Coat: long, dense. Color: shades of lustrous gold.

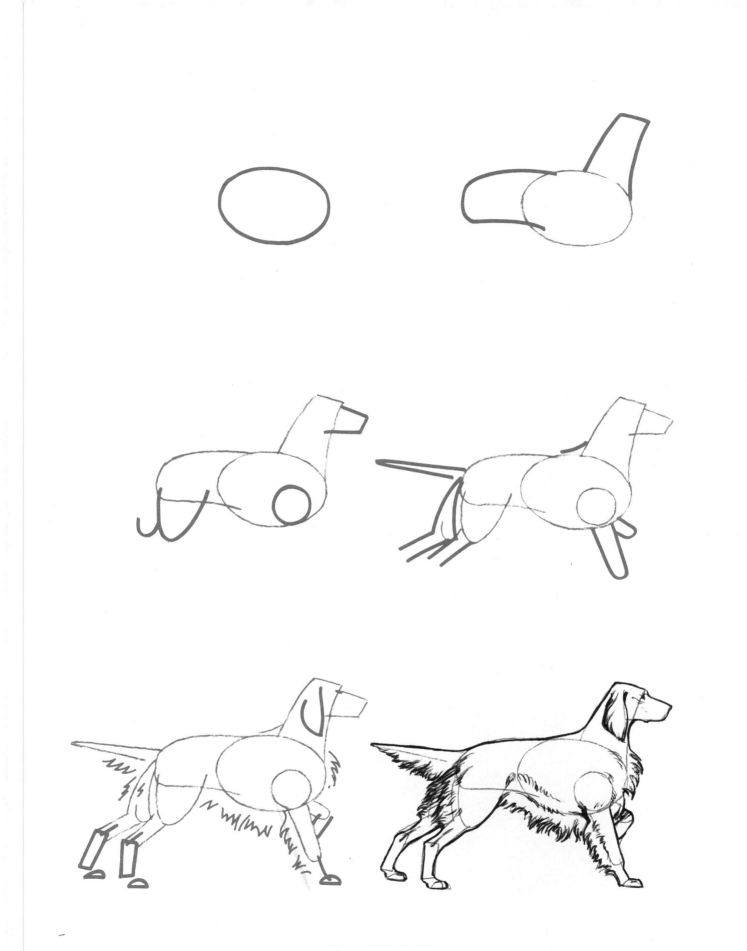

IRISH SETTER

Bred in the Emerald Isle in the 18th century, brought to America in early 1870s. Av. wt. 65 lbs., ht. 25″. Coat: long, straight with fringes. Color: deep rich mahogany, chestnut, red.

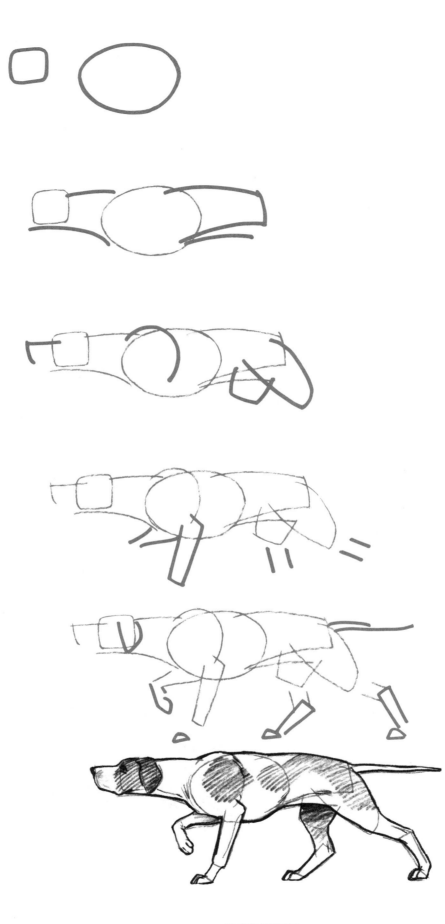

POINTER

Traces ancestry to Spanish pointers brought to England about 1650. Popular in America since 1876. Av. wt. 65 lbs., ht. 25″. Coat: short, flat. Color: white with black, liver, orange or lemon.

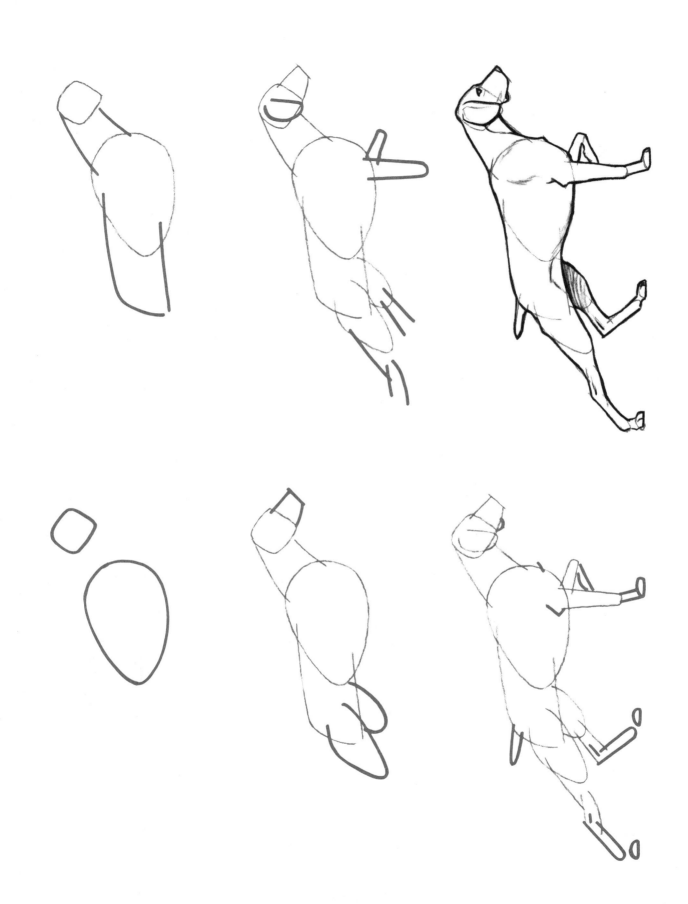

WEIMARANER
Developed in the 1800s at the Court of Weimar, Germany. Originally used on big game. Rapid growth in America since 1929. Av. wt. 75 lbs., ht. 26″. Coat: smooth. Color: solid gray.

The Non-sporting Breeds

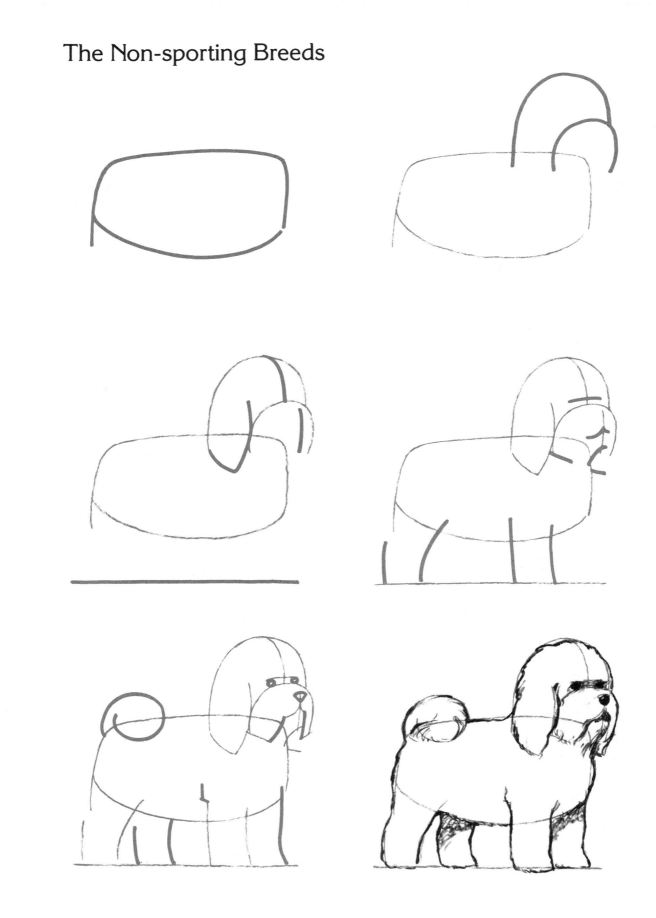

BICHON FRISÉ
Native of Tenerife, largest of Canary Islands. Name means "curly lap dog." Admitted to American Kennel Club 1972. Av. wt. 9 lbs., ht. 10″. Coat: silky, profuse, curled. Color: solid white or with cream, apricot touches.

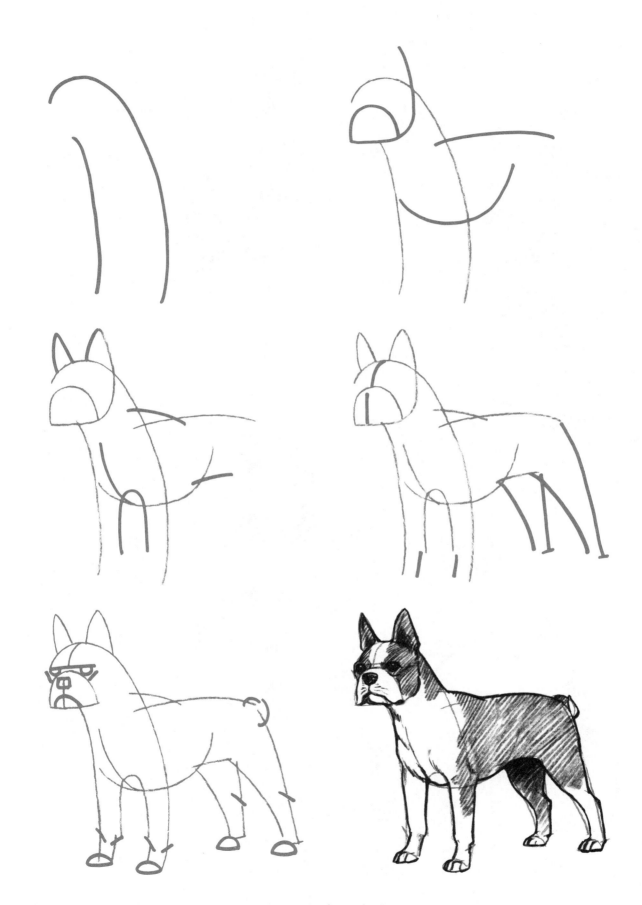

BOSTON TERRIER
Native American breed, developed around Boston in 1875; among most popular ever since.
Av. wt. 19 lbs., ht. 14″. Coat: smooth, glossy. Color: brindle, black, white markings.

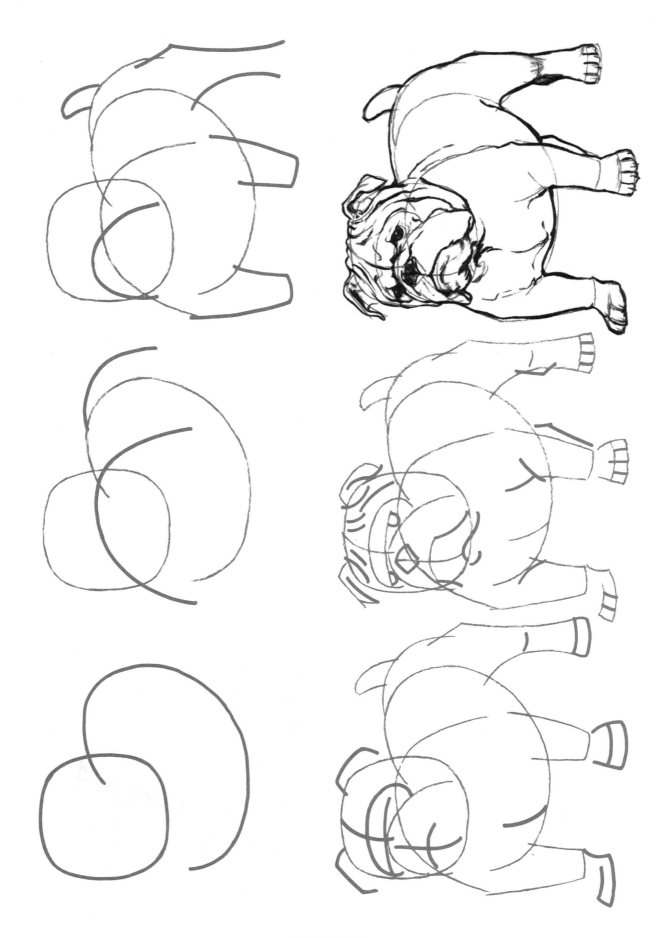

BULLDOG

Symbol of British courage and tenacity world over, but known for gentleness also. Originally used for bullbaiting. Av. wt. 50 lbs., ht. 15″. Coat: short, flat. Color: brindle, white, tan.

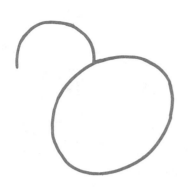
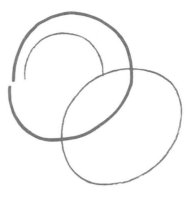
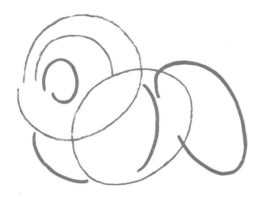
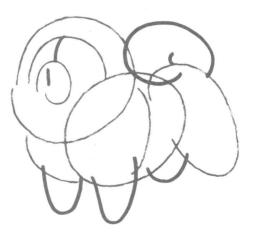
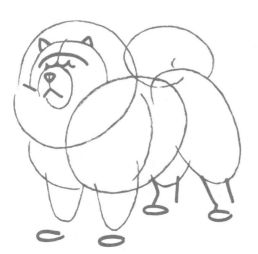
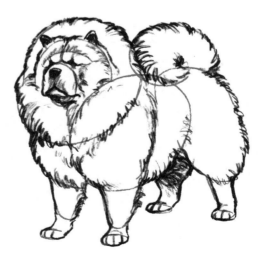

CHOW CHOW
Known in its native China for over 2000 years as a hunter. First imported to U.S. in 1890. Av. wt.
60 lbs., ht. 20″. Coat: abundant. Color: usually red or black, but any solid color.

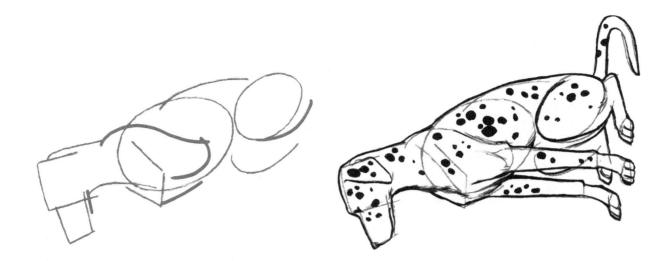

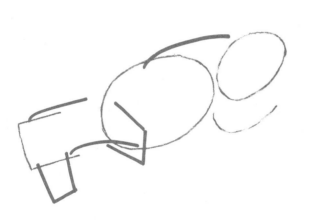

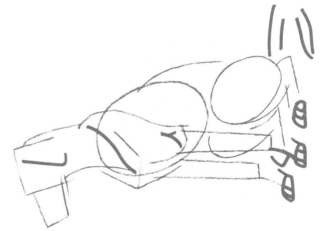

DALMATIAN
From Adriatic province of Dalmatia. Known as coach or fire dog from running with carriages or fire engines. Av. wt. 45 lbs., ht. 21″. Coat: short, sleek. Color: black or liver spotted.

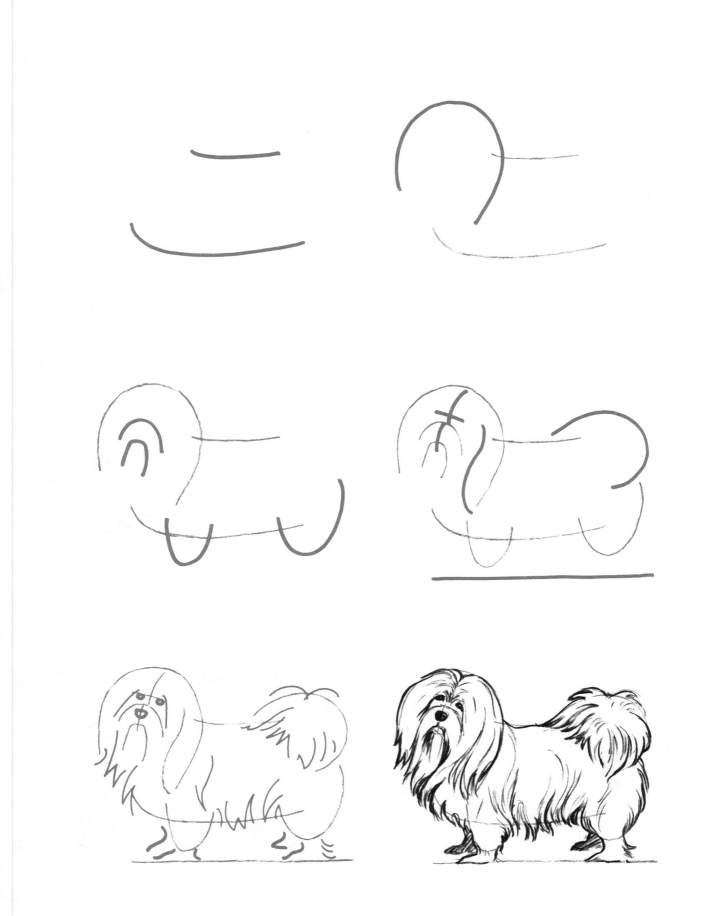

LHASA APSO

Native of Tibet for over 800 years as nobles' watchdog. Short-legged, heavy-coated. Av. wt. 15 lbs., ht. 10″. Coat: heavy, bearded. Color: black to white, with golden preferred.

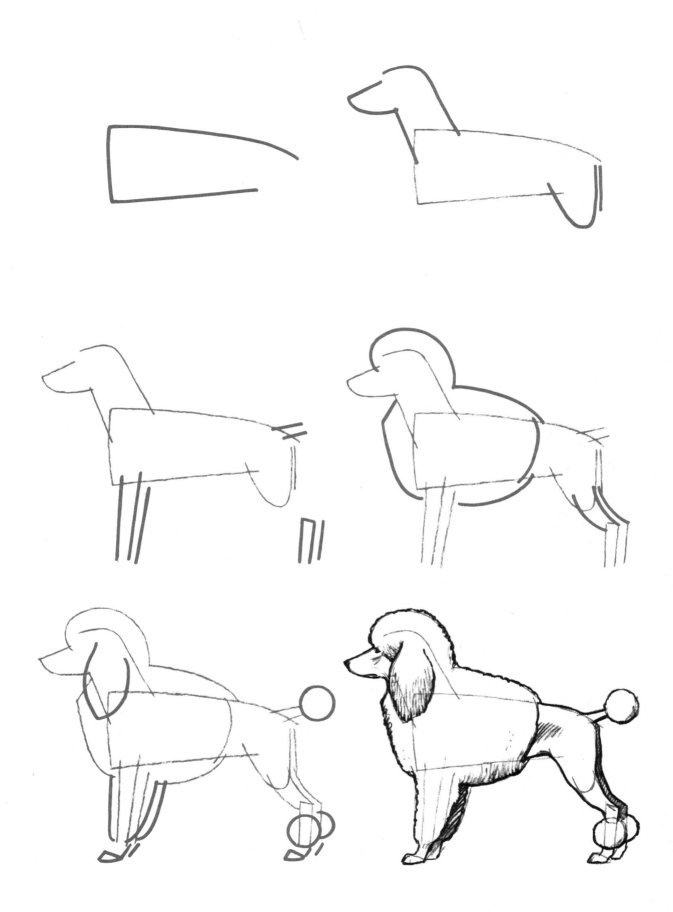

STANDARD POODLE
National dog of France, actually descended from German Pudel. Retriever and circus dog.
Av. wt. 55 lbs., ht. 23″. Color: solid black, white, silver, gray, apricot, brown.

The Toy Breeds

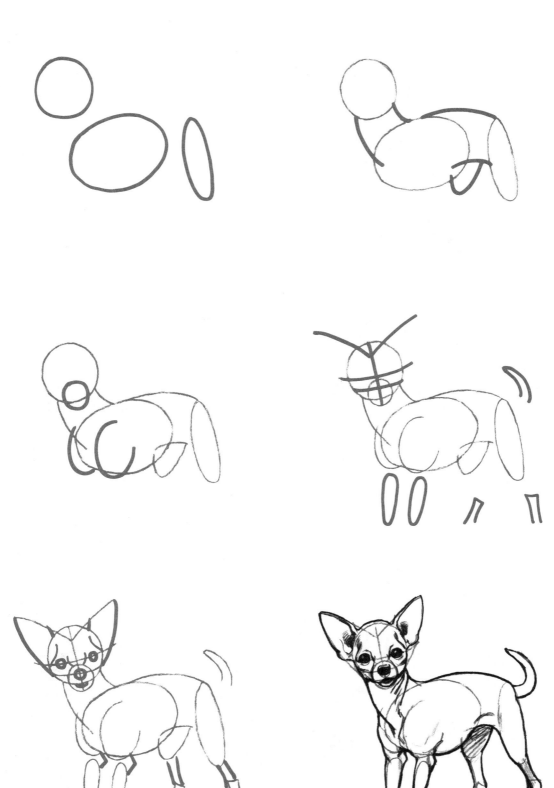

CHIHUAHUA
Smooth coat, similar to the long-coated variety, but with short, glossy hair. Large bat ears, distinctive. Av. wt. 4 lbs., ht. 5″. Color: fawn, red, black and tan, spashed, blue.

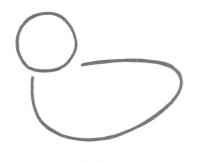
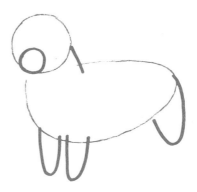
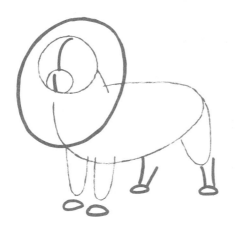
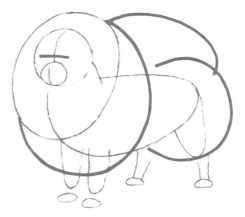
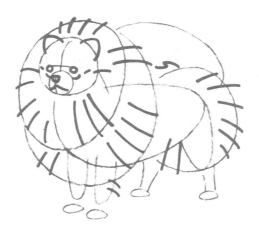
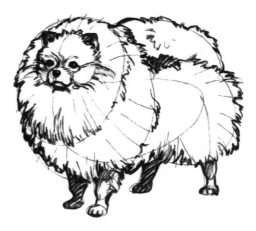

POMERANIAN
Miniature copy of Baltic sled dog; boldness belies size. Av. wt. 5 lbs., ht. 7″. Coat: profuse, curled
tail bushy. Color: orange to black, white, parti-color.

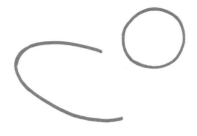
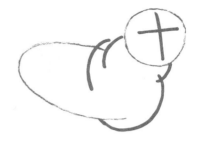

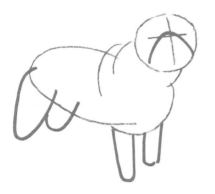
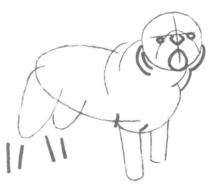

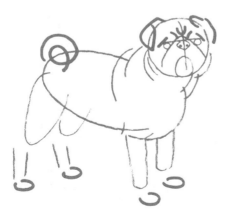
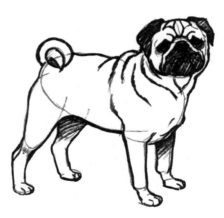

PUG
Originally from China, brought to West from Dutch East Indies. Victorian favorite. Av. wt. 16 lbs.,
ht. 10″. Coat: short, smooth. Color: fawn, with dark face, solid black.

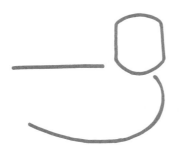
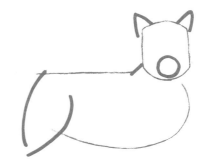
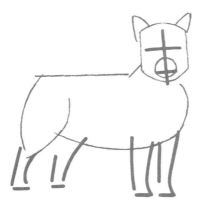
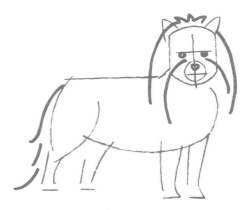
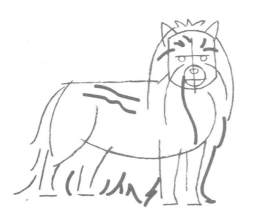
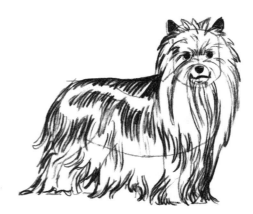

YORKSHIRE TERRIER
Developed in England 100 years ago. Av. wt. 6 lbs., ht. 8″. Coat: long, silky, parted down black like Skye, Maltese. Color: steel blue; tan head and legs.

Lee J. Ames began his career at the Walt Disney Studios, working on films that included *Fantasia* and *Pinocchio*. He taught at the School of Visual Arts in Manhattan, and at Dowling College on Long Island, New York. An avid worker, Ames directed his own advertising agency, illustrated for several magazines, and illustrated approximately 150 books that range from picture books to postgraduate texts. He resided in Dix Hills, Long Island, with his wife, Jocelyn, until his death in June 2011.

DRAW 50 DOGS

Experience All That the Draw 50 Series Has to Offer!

With this proven, step-by-step method, Lee J. Ames has taught millions how to draw everything from amphibians to automobiles. Now it's your turn! Pick up the pencil, get out some paper, and learn how to draw everything under the sun with the Draw 50 series.

Also Available:

- *Draw 50 Animal 'Toons*
- *Draw 50 Animals*
- *Draw 50 Athletes*
- *Draw 50 Baby Animals*
- *Draw 50 Cars, Trucks, and Motorcycles*
- *Draw 50 Cats*
- *Draw 50 Dinosaurs and Other Prehistoric Animals*
- *Draw 50 Famous Cartoons*
- *Draw 50 Flowers, Trees, and Other Plants*
- *Draw 50 Horses*
- *Draw 50 Monsters*
- *Draw 50 People*
- *Draw 50 Princesses*
- *Draw 50 Sharks, Whales, and Other Sea Creatures*
- *Draw 50 Vehicles*
- *Draw the Draw 50 Way*